# teach me about

# Security Objects

Childrens Press
School and Library Edition
Published 1987

Managing Editor: Marilyn Berry
Copy Editor: Orly Kelly
Contributing Writer: Kathleen McBride
Contributing Editors: Georgiana Burt, Radhika Miller
Design and Production: Abigail Johnston
Illustrator: Bartholomew
Composition: Curt Chelin

# teach me about

# Security Objects

*Illustrated by Bartholomew*

CHILDRENS PRESS ®

CHICAGO

I have a favorite thing.

My favorite thing may be a pacifier.

It may be a bottle.

It may be my blanket.

It may be my pillow.

Or, it may be a toy.

I like my favorite thing very much.

I like the way it smells.

I like the way it feels.

9

I like to use my favorite thing.

It makes me feel good.

I usually take my favorite thing

wherever I go.

I am happy when I have it with me.

13

I want my favorite thing near me

whenever I am upset.

It makes me feel better.

15

Sometimes my favorite thing

gets dirty.

It needs to be cleaned.

I cannot have my favorite thing

while it is being cleaned.

Sometimes I must put

my favorite thing aside

while I do something else.

19

Sometimes I lose my favorite thing.

I get very upset.

I look for it.

I find it.

I feel better.

21

When I get bigger,

I will do many things.

I will slide down the slide.

I will climb on the jungle gym.

I will ride a tricycle.

I will play with other children.

It will be hard for me

to do these things

if I am carrying my favorite thing.

23

When I get bigger,

I will not use my favorite thing

all of the time.

I will do other things instead.

25

When I get bigger,

I will go to school.

There will be many things

for me to do.

I will not need to take

my favorite thing.

I will leave it at home.

I will put my favorite thing away

when I stop using it.

I will put it in a special place.

I will keep it forever.

When I am grown up,

it will remind me of what

it was like to be little.

29

It is always nice

to have a favorite thing.

I will probably choose a new one

after I put my old one away.